Cape Cod

Travel Guide

Your Ultimate Companion to Unforgettable Adventures, Scenic Beauty and Coastal Charm

Tyler Rivers

Disclaimer

The pictures featured in this book are for artistic purposes only and do not necessarily represent the actual locations referenced in the text. While every effort has been made to ensure the accuracy of the information contained in this guide, neither the author nor the publisher assumes any responsibility for errors or omissions, or for any consequences arising from the use of the information contained herein.

Table of Content

CHAPTER 1

INTRODUCTION

Welcome to Cape Cod

Nestled along the eastern coast of Massachusetts, Cape Cod is a captivating destination that beckons travelers with its natural beauty, charming towns, and rich maritime history. As you set foot on this iconic peninsula, you'll be greeted by sandy shores, lapping waves, and the invigorating scent of salty sea air. Whether you're seeking a peaceful retreat, outdoor adventures, cultural experiences, or simply a break from the bustling city life, Cape Cod has something special in store for every visitor.

About This Guide

This comprehensive Cape Cod Travel Guide has been carefully crafted to be your go-to companion throughout your journey on the Cape. Our aim is to provide you with all the information you need to plan a memorable trip, making the most of your time in this enchanting region.

In this guide, you'll find details about the must-visit attractions, top accommodation options, delectable dining spots, exciting outdoor activities, cultural highlights, shopping destinations, and much more.

We've also included recommended itineraries to suit different interests and travel durations, ensuring you get the best experience possible.

How to Use This Guide

To make the most of this guide, we recommend starting with the "Getting to Cape Cod" section, where you'll find various transportation options, including how to reach the Cape by air, car, train, or bus. This section will help you plan your journey to Cape Cod seamlessly.

Next, explore the "Where to Visit in Cape Cod" chapter, where we highlight the most captivating spots that define the essence of the Cape. From the pristine beaches of Cape Cod National Seashore to the vibrant streets of Provincetown and the charming town of Chatham, each destination has a unique allure waiting to be discovered.

Once you've decided on the places you want to explore, move on to the "Accommodation Options" section. Here, we've curated a selection of luxury resorts, cozy bed and breakfasts, and beachfront rentals to cater to different preferences and budgets, ensuring a comfortable stay throughout your vacation.

Indulge your taste buds with the diverse "Dining and Local Cuisine" chapter, featuring Cape Cod's seafood specialties and the top restaurants and cafes that offer delectable meals. Treat yourself to the freshest seafood, traditional clam chowder, and scrumptious lobster rolls for an unforgettable culinary experience.

If you're an outdoor enthusiast, head straight to the "Outdoor Activities and Recreation" section, where you'll find information about beach activities, biking trails, nature hikes, birdwatching spots, and golf courses that will keep you active and immersed in nature during your stay.

Immerse yourself in the arts and culture of Cape Cod through the "Arts and Culture" chapter, which showcases the region's art museums, theaters, and performing arts centers. Discover Cape Cod's vibrant artistic community and witness captivating performances that reflect the area's rich cultural heritage.

For those eager to indulge in retail therapy, the "Shopping in Cape Cod" chapter offers insights into unique boutiques, art galleries, and shopping centers, where you can find one-of-a-kind souvenirs and treasures to take back home.

If you're traveling with furry companions, don't miss the "Traveling with Pets" section, which provides details on pet-friendly beaches, accommodations, and local pet services, ensuring a memorable vacation for both you and your four-legged friends.

Safety is paramount during any trip, and we've included an informative "Safety and Emergency Information" section that outlines essential contacts, medical facilities, and weather-related tips to keep you well-prepared during your stay.

As responsible travelers, we encourage you to explore the "Sustainable Travel Tips" chapter, which suggests eco-friendly practices and activities that support conservation efforts and reduce your environmental impact while exploring this pristine destination.

Essential Tips for Traveling to Cape Cod

Before you embark on your Cape Cod adventure, we've compiled a set of essential tips to ensure you have a smooth and enjoyable experience:

a. **Pack Sunscreen**: Cape Cod enjoys sunny days throughout the year, so don't forget to pack sunscreen, sunglasses, and a wide-brimmed hat to protect yourself from the sun's rays.

b. **Embrace Layering**: Cape Cod's weather can be unpredictable, especially near the coast. Pack layers to stay comfortable, including light jackets or sweaters, even during the summer months.

c. **Check for Seasonal Events**: Cape Cod hosts numerous festivals and events throughout the year. Before your trip, check the local events calendar to see if any festivities align with your travel dates.

d. **Respect Wildlife and Nature**: Cape Cod's natural beauty is home to diverse wildlife. Please observe animals from a safe distance and adhere to any conservation guidelines in place.

e. **Book Accommodations in Advance**: Especially during peak seasons, Cape Cod can get crowded. It's advisable to book your accommodations well in advance to secure your preferred stay.

f. **Bring Bug Repellent**: While Cape Cod is generally pleasant, mosquitoes can be active during certain times of the year. Carry insect repellent to keep the bugs at bay.

Now that you're equipped with essential knowledge, let your Cape Cod adventure begin! Flip through the following chapters to uncover the treasures this peninsula has to offer. Discover the beauty of Cape Cod's natural landscapes, immerse yourself in its rich culture, and create unforgettable memories that will last a lifetime. Happy travels!

CHAPTER 2

GETTING TO CAPE COD

Cape Cod, with its pristine beaches, charming towns, and rich maritime heritage, is a popular vacation destination on the East Coast of the United States. Whether you're arriving from nearby cities or distant states, there are several convenient ways to access this beautiful peninsula. In this chapter, we'll explore the various transportation options available to travelers and provide essential tips for getting around Cape Cod once you're there.

By Air

Cape Cod is served by several airports, making it easily accessible for both domestic and international travelers. The two main airports that cater to Cape Cod visitors are:

1. Barnstable Municipal Airport (HYA): Located in Hyannis, this regional airport is the closest to the heart of Cape Cod. It offers daily flights from major cities such as Boston, New York, and Nantucket. From Barnstable Municipal Airport, you can rent a car, take a taxi, or use public transportation to reach your final destination.

2. Logan International Airport (BOS): Situated in Boston, Logan Airport is the largest airport in the region and offers a wide range of domestic and international flights. While it's farther from Cape Cod than Barnstable Municipal Airport, it provides more flight options. After landing at Logan, you can rent a car or take a shuttle service to Cape Cod.

By Car

Driving to Cape Cod is a popular option for those who prefer the flexibility of having their own vehicle during their stay. The region is well-connected to major highways, making road trips a convenient and scenic way to reach your destination.

From Boston: If you're coming from Boston, take Interstate 93 South to Route 3 South, and then follow the signs for the Sagamore Bridge, which connects the mainland to Cape Cod.

From Providence: Travelers from Providence can take Interstate 195 East, which leads directly to Cape Cod via the Bourne Bridge.

From New York and Connecticut: Those arriving from New York or Connecticut can take Interstate 95 North to Interstate 195 East, eventually reaching the Bourne Bridge.

During the peak summer months, especially on weekends, traffic can be heavy on the bridges, so plan your travel accordingly and consider traveling during non-peak hours if possible.

By Train or Bus

While Cape Cod doesn't have its own train station, you can still reach the area by rail through Amtrak or regional trains. Amtrak's Boston South Station is well-connected to major cities along the East Coast, and from there, you can transfer to local trains or buses to get to Cape Cod.

Alternatively, several bus companies offer routes to Cape Cod from Boston and other nearby cities. These buses provide a cost-effective option for travelers who prefer public transportation.

Getting Around Cape Cod

Once you've arrived in Cape Cod, you'll need a reliable way to explore the various towns, beaches, and attractions. Here are the primary transportation options available within the region:

1. Car Rental: Renting a car is a popular choice for visitors who want the freedom to explore at their own pace.

Numerous car rental agencies operate in Cape Cod, and you can choose from a variety of vehicle types to suit your needs.

2. Cape Cod Regional Transit Authority (CCRTA): The CCRTA operates an extensive public transportation network throughout Cape Cod. Buses run on fixed routes, making stops at key locations, including popular beaches and towns. The CCRTA buses are an affordable and eco-friendly way to travel around the area.

3. Taxis and Ride-Sharing Services: Taxis are available in most towns, and ride-sharing services like Uber and Lyft also operate in the region. These options are convenient for short trips or when you don't want to drive yourself.

4. Biking: Cape Cod is a bike-friendly destination, with numerous scenic bike trails and paths. Many towns offer bike rentals, and exploring the area on two wheels allows you to enjoy the beautiful coastal scenery up close.

5. Ferries: If you're staying in or near Hyannis, ferries provide a unique way to visit Martha's Vineyard and Nantucket, two other popular destinations in the area.

The ferries offer stunning views of the ocean and are an exciting addition to your Cape Cod experience.

CHAPTER 3

WHERE TO VISIT IN CAPE COD

Cape Cod, with its pristine beaches, charming towns, and rich maritime history, offers a plethora of captivating destinations for travelers to explore. In this chapter, we will delve into some of the must-visit places on the Cape, each offering a unique experience that will undoubtedly leave a lasting impression.

Cape Cod National Seashore

One of the crown jewels of Cape Cod is undoubtedly the Cape Cod National Seashore. Encompassing over 40 miles of coastline, this protected area showcases the region's natural beauty and offers an array of outdoor activities. Within the seashore, visitors can find numerous stunning beaches, each with its distinct character.

1. Coast Guard Beach

Coast Guard Beach, located in Eastham, consistently ranks as one of the top beaches in the United States. Its vast stretch of sandy shoreline and picturesque dunes make it a favorite among locals and tourists alike. Swimmers and sunbathers can relax in the warm summer sun, while adventurous souls can take a refreshing dip in the Atlantic Ocean. Nature enthusiasts will appreciate the scenic nature trails that wind through the surrounding dunes and marshlands, providing excellent opportunities for birdwatching.

2. Marconi Beach

Named after Guglielmo Marconi, the inventor of the wireless telegraph, Marconi Beach in Wellfleet offers not only a stunning seascape but also a historical touch. The site is where Marconi first demonstrated transatlantic wireless communication in 1903. Today, visitors can marvel at the same vast ocean views that once connected continents. The beach's steep dunes provide an excellent vantage point for capturing breathtaking sunsets, and the rolling waves make it a popular spot for surfers.

3. Race Point Beach

Race Point Beach, situated in Provincetown, is renowned for its wild and rugged beauty. Part of the seashore's northernmost tip, it is an ideal destination for those seeking solitude and a sense of untamed nature. The area is a prime location for spotting whales during their migratory seasons, making it a favorite among whale watchers.

Hiking trails along the shoreline and through the adjacent dunes offer an opportunity to connect with nature and enjoy breathtaking panoramic views of the ocean.

Provincetown

Provincetown, affectionately known as P-town, is a vibrant and colorful town located at the very tip of Cape Cod. Famous for its artsy and welcoming atmosphere, Provincetown has long been a haven for artists, writers, and the LGBTQ+ community.

1. Pilgrim Monument

Dominating Provincetown's skyline, the Pilgrim Monument stands as a symbol of the town's history. It commemorates the Pilgrims' first landing in Provincetown in 1620 before they eventually settled in Plymouth. Visitors can climb the monument's 252-foot tower for breathtaking panoramic views of the Cape and the Atlantic Ocean.

2. Commercial Street

The heart of Provincetown is undoubtedly Commercial Street. Lined with boutiques, art galleries, restaurants, and bars, this bustling thoroughfare offers a delightful mix of shopping, dining, and entertainment.

Visitors can browse unique artworks, pick up souvenirs, or savor delicious seafood dishes while enjoying the vibrant street atmosphere.

3. Whale Watching Tours

Provincetown is widely regarded as one of the best whale watching destinations on the East Coast. Several companies offer whale watching tours that take visitors offshore to observe humpback, minke, and finback whales, among others, in their natural habitat. These majestic creatures grace the waters from spring to fall, providing an awe-inspiring and educational experience for visitors of all ages.

Chatham

Chatham, an elegant town located on the southeastern tip of Cape Cod, boasts a rich maritime heritage and a quaint New England charm.

1. Chatham Lighthouse

The Chatham Lighthouse, perched on the edge of Chatham's Main Beach, is an iconic symbol of the town. The present lighthouse, built in 1877, replaced the original structure that was moved due to erosion. Visitors can tour the lighthouse, learn about its history, and enjoy stunning views of the Atlantic Ocean and Chatham Harbor.

2. Main Street Shopping

Chatham's Main Street is a quintessential New England setting with its tree-lined sidewalks, charming boutiques, and art galleries. Shoppers can browse a variety of shops offering unique jewelry, clothing, and home decor items. The street is also home to quaint cafes and restaurants, perfect for a leisurely lunch or afternoon tea.

3.Monomoy National Wildlife Refuge

Nature lovers should not miss the opportunity to explore the Monomoy National Wildlife Refuge. This protected area comprises pristine salt marshes, dunes, and barrier beaches, providing critical habitat for migratory birds and marine wildlife. Guided tours and birdwatching excursions are available for those interested in learning more about the local flora and fauna.

Hyannis

As the largest town on Cape Cod, Hyannis is a bustling hub that offers a mix of history, culture, and maritime experiences.

1. John F. Kennedy Hyannis Museum

Hyannis holds a special place in American history as the beloved summer home of the Kennedy family. The John F. Kennedy Hyannis Museum pays tribute to the legacy of President John F. Kennedy and his family's time on Cape Cod. Visitors can explore exhibits that chronicle the Kennedys' life and connection to the Cape.

2. Hyannis Harbor

Hyannis Harbor is a picturesque waterfront area bustling with activity. Stroll along the docks to observe fishing boats and yachts or embark on a relaxing harbor cruise. The harbor also serves as a departure point for ferries to the nearby islands of Nantucket and Martha's Vineyard, offering a convenient opportunity for island-hopping adventures.

3. Cape Cod Maritime Museum

For a deeper understanding of Cape Cod's maritime history, the Cape Cod Maritime Museum is a must-visit.

This interactive museum showcases the region's seafaring heritage through exhibits, workshops, and events. Visitors can learn about traditional boatbuilding, explore maritime art, and even try their hand at sailing in the museum's small craft center.

Cape Cod's diverse destinations offer something for every traveler, from nature enthusiasts to history buffs, art lovers, and beachgoers. With its unique blend of coastal charm and cultural richness, Cape Cod promises an unforgettable experience that will leave visitors longing to return again and again.

CHAPTER 4

ACCOMMODATION OPTIONS

Cape Cod offers a diverse range of accommodation options to suit every traveler's preference and budget. From luxurious resorts with breathtaking ocean views to charming bed and breakfasts nestled in picturesque towns, and cozy beachfront cottages, there's something for everyone. In this chapter, we will explore some of the best places to stay in Cape Cod, ensuring you have a comfortable and memorable stay during your visit to this beautiful destination.

Luxury Resorts and Hotels

If you're looking for a lavish and pampering experience, Cape Cod's luxury resorts and hotels are the perfect choice. These establishments offer top-notch amenities, world-class service, and stunning locations along the coast.

1. The Chatham Bars Inn

Located in the charming town of Chatham, The Chatham Bars Inn is an iconic and elegant resort that has been welcoming guests since 1914. Situated on a private beach, this historic property boasts luxurious rooms and suites with spectacular ocean views.

The resort offers a full range of amenities, including a private golf course, spa, tennis courts, and multiple dining options serving delectable seafood and New England specialties.

2. Wequassett Resort and Golf Club

Nestled on Pleasant Bay in Harwich, Wequassett Resort and Golf Club is a premier luxury resort known for its refined elegance and natural beauty. The resort features luxurious rooms and suites, many of which offer private balconies with captivating water views. Guests can indulge in various recreational activities, including sailing, kayaking, and golfing at the neighboring championship golf course. The on-site restaurants offer gourmet dining experiences with a focus on fresh, locally sourced ingredients.

3. The Ocean Edge Resort and Golf Club

Situated in Brewster, The Ocean Edge Resort and Golf Club is a sprawling property spanning 429 acres and offering access to a private beach on Cape Cod Bay. The resort provides an array of accommodation options, including spacious villas and charming rooms in the historic mansion. With multiple pools, tennis courts, and a Nicklaus-designed golf course, guests can enjoy an active and luxurious stay. The on-site restaurants offer delicious meals with a touch of Cape Cod's culinary delights.

Cozy Bed and Breakfasts

For a more intimate and personalized experience, Cape Cod's bed and breakfasts (B&Bs) offer a warm and welcoming ambiance, often hosted by friendly innkeepers who can provide insider tips and recommendations.

1. Captain's House Inn

Located in Chatham, Captain's House Inn is a beautifully restored sea captain's mansion dating back to 1839. This elegant B&B exudes historic charm with modern comforts. Each room is uniquely decorated with period furnishings, and guests are treated to a gourmet breakfast each morning. The lush gardens and serene outdoor patio offer a relaxing atmosphere for a peaceful escape.

2. The Inn at Cook Street

Situated in the heart of Provincetown, The Inn at Cook Street is a charming B&B known for its Victorian architecture and delightful hospitality. The inn features cozy rooms and suites, some with fireplaces and private balconies. Guests can enjoy a delicious homemade breakfast and take advantage of the inn's proximity to Provincetown's art galleries, shops, and restaurants.

3. The Palmer House Inn

Located in the historic district of Falmouth, The Palmer House Inn is a romantic B&B housed in a 1901 Victorian home. The inn offers elegant rooms with antique furnishings and modern amenities. Guests can savor a gourmet breakfast in the sunny dining room or relax in the beautiful garden courtyard. The Palmer House Inn provides easy access to Falmouth's Main Street and its charming boutiques and eateries.

Beachfront Cottages and Rentals

For those seeking a home-away-from-home experience, renting a beachfront cottage is an excellent option. Cape Cod offers numerous vacation rentals that provide direct access to the sandy shores and stunning ocean views.

1. Sea Mist Resort

Situated in Mashpee, Sea Mist Resort offers cozy cottages and townhouses overlooking Nantucket Sound. Guests can enjoy access to a private beach, indoor and outdoor pools, and other recreational facilities. The cottages come equipped with fully equipped kitchens, making it ideal for families and extended stays.

2. Cape Cod Ocean Manor

Located in Dennis Port, Cape Cod Ocean Manor offers beachfront vacation rentals with a laid-back atmosphere. The property features spacious cottages with full kitchens, private patios, and direct beach access. It's the perfect spot for a relaxing beach vacation with family or friends.

3. Beach Plum Cottages

Situated in North Truro near Provincetown, Beach Plum Cottages offer charming and rustic accommodations nestled among sand dunes. The cottages are equipped with basic amenities, and guests can enjoy a tranquil setting just steps away from the beach. The stunning sunsets over Cape Cod Bay are an unforgettable highlight of a stay at Beach Plum Cottages.

No matter which type of accommodation you choose, staying in Cape Cod will surely leave you with fond memories of this enchanting destination. From luxury resorts to cozy bed and breakfasts or charming beachfront cottages, the variety of options ensures that your stay is tailored to your preferences, making your trip to Cape Cod truly unforgettable.

CHAPTER 5

DINING AND LOCAL CUISINE

When visiting Cape Cod, one cannot miss the opportunity to indulge in its delectable seafood specialties and experience the vibrant local culinary scene. With an abundance of fresh seafood caught daily, Cape Cod's restaurants and eateries offer a delightful array of dishes that will tantalize your taste buds. In this chapter, we will explore some of the must-try seafood delicacies, highlight the top restaurants and cafes, and guide you on a culinary journey that will leave you craving for more.

Cape Cod Seafood Specialties

Cape Cod's rich maritime heritage and access to the Atlantic Ocean make it a seafood lover's paradise. The region is renowned for its fresh catches, and three seafood specialties stand out as iconic delicacies:

1. Clam Chowder

No trip to Cape Cod is complete without savoring a bowl of traditional New England Clam Chowder. This creamy soup is a comforting blend of fresh clams, potatoes, onions, salted pork, and cream. The clams add a subtly sweet and briny flavor to the soup, while the potatoes provide a satisfying texture. Many restaurants and clam shacks across the Cape proudly serve their own versions of this classic dish, and each one offers a unique twist on the beloved recipe.

2. Lobster Roll

A Cape Cod visit demands a taste of the famous Lobster Roll. Succulent chunks of tender lobster meat are mixed with just the right amount of mayonnaise, butter, or both, and served in a buttered and toasted split-top roll. The result is a heavenly marriage of flavors and textures that celebrate the essence of Cape Cod's coastal charm. Whether you prefer a classic cold lobster roll or a warm, buttery version, you'll find this iconic dish at numerous seafood shacks and fine dining establishments throughout the Cape.

3. Wellfleet Oysters

Wellfleet, a picturesque town on Cape Cod, is renowned for its succulent oysters. These briny bivalves are cultivated in the town's nutrient-rich waters, which imparts a distinctive flavor unique to Wellfleet oysters. The raw oysters are often served on the half shell, allowing you to savor the fresh taste of the sea. Many local restaurants and oyster farms offer oyster tours and tastings, providing a memorable experience for seafood enthusiasts.

Top Restaurants and Cafes

Cape Cod's culinary landscape is diverse, offering a range of dining options that cater to various tastes and preferences. Whether you're seeking a casual seaside shack experience or an elegant waterfront meal, Cape Cod has something to satisfy every palate.

1. The Lobster Pot

Located in Provincetown, The Lobster Pot has been a staple of the Cape Cod dining scene since 1979. This family-owned restaurant offers an extensive seafood menu, with dishes prepared using the freshest local ingredients. The Lobster Pot's waterfront location allows guests to enjoy stunning views while relishing their meals. Don't miss their award-winning clam chowder or the famous lobster bisque for an unforgettable taste of Cape Cod.

2. The Red Inn

Situated in Provincetown, The Red Inn is a historic waterfront inn and restaurant with a reputation for elegant dining experiences. Offering panoramic views of Provincetown Harbor, this upscale eatery features a refined menu that highlights the best of Cape Cod's seafood and seasonal produce.

Their creative dishes, coupled with impeccable service, make The Red Inn an ideal choice for a special occasion or a romantic evening.

3. The Black Cat Tavern

Located in Hyannis, The Black Cat Tavern has been serving locals and visitors alike since 1962. Overlooking Hyannis Harbor, this casual yet inviting restaurant offers a wide selection of seafood dishes, including their famous lobster roll. With indoor and outdoor seating options, patrons can enjoy the laid-back atmosphere and watch boats sail in and out of the harbor while enjoying their meals.

Cape Cod's culinary delights are an essential part of the region's charm and allure. From classic clam chowder and lobster rolls to fresh Wellfleet oysters, each dish tells a tale of Cape Cod's coastal heritage. The top restaurants and cafes not only showcase the finest seafood but also offer stunning views and warm hospitality, making every dining experience a memorable one. Whether you're a seafood enthusiast or simply a curious traveler, exploring Cape Cod's dining scene will undoubtedly be a highlight of your journey. So, come hungry, and let Cape Cod's culinary treasures treat you to an unforgettable gastronomic adventure.

CHAPTER 6

OUTDOOR ACTIVITIES AND RECREATION

Cape Cod offers a plethora of outdoor activities and recreational opportunities that cater to all types of travelers. Whether you prefer basking on sandy shores, exploring nature trails, engaging in thrilling water sports, or playing golf amidst breathtaking landscapes, Cape Cod has something for everyone. This chapter will guide you through the best outdoor adventures the region has to offer.

Beach Activities

Cape Cod's pristine beaches are a major draw for tourists from all around the world. With over 500 miles of coastline, there are plenty of options for sunbathing, swimming, and beachcombing. Each beach has its unique charm and characteristics, and it's worth exploring different ones during your visit.

1. Swimming and Sunbathing

The warm summer months provide the perfect conditions for swimming and sunbathing along Cape Cod's sandy shores. Families with children can find calm waters and gentle waves at beaches like Craigville Beach in Centerville and

Corporation Beach in Dennis. For a more vibrant atmosphere, head to popular beaches like Nauset Beach in Orleans or Coast Guard Beach in Eastham, where you can catch some rays and play beach games with fellow travelers.

2. Surfing and Paddleboarding

Surf enthusiasts flock to Cape Cod for its excellent waves and surfing opportunities. Coast Guard Beach, Marconi Beach, and White Crest Beach in Wellfleet are known for their impressive surf breaks, making them ideal spots for experienced surfers. If you're new to the sport, many local surf schools offer lessons and equipment rentals to help you catch your first wave.

For a calmer water experience, try paddleboarding along the tranquil estuaries and salt marshes. Places like Pleasant Bay and Bass River are perfect for paddleboarding, providing a peaceful way to explore the region's rich natural beauty.

3. Beach Bonfires

As the sun sets over Cape Cod's horizon, beach bonfires become a delightful way to unwind and create lasting memories with family and friends. Several beaches, such as Race Point Beach in Provincetown and Mayflower Beach in Dennis, allow bonfires with proper permits.

Gather around the crackling fire, roast marshmallows, and enjoy the captivating starry sky above.

Biking Trails

Cape Cod boasts scenic biking trails that meander through picturesque landscapes, charming towns, and wildlife sanctuaries. Exploring the region on two wheels offers a unique perspective and a chance to embrace the natural splendor.

1. Cape Cod Rail Trail

The Cape Cod Rail Trail is a popular biking route stretching 22 miles from South Dennis to Wellfleet. This well-maintained trail follows the path of a former railroad and passes through lush forests, quaint towns, and serene lakes. Bikers of all levels can enjoy this trail, and it's a great activity for families too. Don't forget to pack a picnic and take breaks at scenic spots along the way.

2. Shining Sea Bikeway

For a coastal biking experience, head to Falmouth and ride along the Shining Sea Bikeway. This 10.7-mile trail offers breathtaking views of the ocean and takes you through salt marshes and cranberry bogs.

The trail's name is inspired by the line from the song "America the Beautiful" penned by Falmouth native Katharine Lee Bates. With plenty of benches and observation areas, you can take leisurely breaks and appreciate the stunning vistas.

Nature Hiking and Birdwatching

Cape Cod is a haven for nature enthusiasts and birdwatchers. Numerous nature reserves and wildlife sanctuaries provide opportunities to explore diverse ecosystems and observe various bird species.

1. Wellfleet Bay Wildlife Sanctuary

Managed by Mass Audubon, the Wellfleet Bay Wildlife Sanctuary is a must-visit for birdwatching and nature walks. The sanctuary features five miles of trails that wind through salt marshes, woodlands, and sandy beaches. Keep an eye out for migratory birds, such as Piping Plovers and Roseate Terns, that frequent the area during the breeding season.

2. Nickerson State Park

Nickerson State Park, located in Brewster, offers an extensive trail network, perfect for hikers of all skill levels. The park's diverse landscapes include forests, ponds, and kettle ponds created by retreating glaciers thousands of years ago.

Nature lovers will find an abundance of wildlife and native flora while exploring the park's 1900 acres.

Golf Courses

Cape Cod's golf courses are a golfer's paradise, offering scenic backdrops and challenging layouts for players of all abilities. Whether you're a seasoned golfer or just looking to enjoy a leisurely round, Cape Cod's golf courses won't disappoint.

1. Highland Links Golf Course

Located in North Truro, Highland Links Golf Course is one of the most scenic and historic courses on Cape Cod. Perched atop the bluffs overlooking the Atlantic Ocean, this public course offers stunning views and a challenging 9-hole layout. The course's history dates back to 1892, making it one of the oldest in the country.

2. Cape Cod National Golf Club

Designed by Jack Nicklaus, the Cape Cod National Golf Club in Brewster is a top-rated private course that has consistently received accolades for its beauty and playability. The club's 18-hole championship course is nestled amid natural landscapes and features water hazards, bunkers, and undulating greens that will test even the most skilled golfers.

Cape Cod's outdoor offerings provide an exceptional blend of relaxation and adventure. From lounging on the beaches to exploring the natural wonders, every moment spent in the great outdoors of Cape Cod will leave you with cherished memories of your journey.

CHAPTER 7

ARTS AND CULTURE

Cape Cod Art Museums

Cape Cod's vibrant arts and culture scene has long been a draw for creative souls and art enthusiasts. The region is home to several exceptional art museums, each offering a unique perspective on the area's rich artistic heritage and contemporary expressions. Whether you are an art aficionado or simply appreciate the beauty of visual arts, visiting these museums is an enriching experience.

1. Cape Cod Museum of Art

Nestled in the quaint town of Dennis, the Cape Cod Museum of Art (CCMoA) is a treasure trove of artistic wonders. As you approach the museum, the picturesque landscape dotted with sculptures welcomes you, setting the tone for what lies ahead. The CCMoA celebrates the works of both historic and contemporary Cape Cod artists, showcasing a diverse collection of paintings, sculptures, photographs, and multimedia installations.

Inside, you'll find thoughtfully curated exhibitions that highlight the region's stunning natural beauty, maritime history, and the profound influence of Cape Cod on the artists who call it home. From the classic seascapes of Edward Hopper to modern abstract compositions, the museum's ever-changing exhibits offer something to captivate every art lover.

One of the museum's highlights is its dedication to fostering local talent through educational programs and community outreach. Visitors can participate in workshops, art classes, and lectures, gaining insights into various art forms and techniques. If you're lucky, you might catch an artist-in-residence at work, providing a unique opportunity to witness the creative process firsthand.

2. Heritage Museums & Gardens

While not exclusively an art museum, the Heritage Museums & Gardens in Sandwich is an enchanting destination that seamlessly weaves together art, horticulture, and history. Set on 100 acres of beautifully landscaped grounds, this living museum boasts an impressive collection of art and artifacts, making it a must-visit on your Cape Cod journey.

Stroll through the gardens adorned with sculptures and outdoor installations, discovering hidden art pieces as you meander along winding paths. The garden's seasonal blooms provide a stunning backdrop for both the artworks and your memorable experience.

The museum's curators carefully integrate art installations, ensuring that the pieces resonate harmoniously with the natural surroundings.

Inside the museum's galleries, you'll find a delightful assortment of American folk art, antique automobiles, and historical artifacts that shed light on Cape Cod's cultural heritage. From handcrafted quilts to intricately carved wooden figures, each item tells a story of the region's past and its people's creativity.

Theatres and Performing Arts Centers

1. Cape Playhouse

The Cape Playhouse, located in Dennis, holds the distinction of being the oldest professional summer theater in the United States. Steeped in history and theatrical tradition, the Cape Playhouse has been graced by the presence of numerous renowned actors and playwrights over the decades.

Entering the quaint theater is like stepping back in time. The iconic red barn-like structure exudes charm and nostalgia, and as the curtains rise, you'll be transported to a world of captivating performances. From classic plays to contemporary dramas and Broadway hits, the Cape

Playhouse's repertoire is diverse, catering to audiences of all ages and tastes.

Attending a show at the Cape Playhouse is an experience like no other. The intimate setting allows you to feel an emotional connection to the actors on stage, enhancing the power of the performances. Before or after the show, take a moment to explore the theater's lobby, adorned with photographs and memorabilia, honoring the illustrious history of this cultural gem.

2. Provincetown Theater

Provincetown, a hub of creativity and inclusivity, boasts its own vibrant performing arts scene, with the Provincetown Theater at its heart. Known for its avant-garde productions, experimental plays, and strong emphasis on LGBTQ+ representation, this theater offers a refreshing and progressive approach to storytelling.

The Provincetown Theater prides itself on being a platform for emerging playwrights and performers, pushing the boundaries of conventional theater. As you step into the theater, you'll be enveloped by an atmosphere of acceptance and open-mindedness, creating a safe space for artists and audience members alike.

The theater's calendar features an array of thought-provoking plays, thoughtfully curated to challenge societal norms and ignite conversations on important issues. Additionally, the Provincetown Theater hosts workshops and events that foster artistic growth and encourage dialogue within the community.

CHAPTER 8

SHOPPING IN CAPE COD

Cape Cod offers a delightful shopping experience for visitors, with a wide array of unique boutiques, art galleries, outlet malls, and shopping centers to explore. Whether you're looking for handcrafted souvenirs, local artwork, fashionable clothing, or charming home decor, you'll find something special to take home with you. This chapter will guide you through the best shopping destinations on the Cape, ensuring you have an enjoyable and fruitful shopping adventure.

Unique Boutiques and Art Galleries

One of the highlights of shopping in Cape Cod is the abundance of charming boutiques and art galleries. Stroll along the picturesque streets of towns like Chatham, Provincetown, and Sandwich, where you'll discover an array of locally-owned shops offering hand-selected items.

In Chatham, you'll find unique boutiques offering coastal-inspired clothing, artisanal jewelry, and nautical-themed home decor. Don't miss the opportunity to explore the Chatham Orpheum Theater's gallery, which showcases works from local artists.

Provincetown, with its vibrant art scene, is a haven for art lovers. The Provincetown Art Association and Museum (PAAM) features a diverse collection of artwork and hosts exhibitions year-round. Along Commercial Street, you'll find numerous art galleries featuring paintings, sculptures, photography, and mixed media creations from both established and up-and-coming artists.

Sandwich, the oldest town on Cape Cod, is home to a variety of charming boutiques offering antique treasures, handcrafted gifts, and unique collectibles. Take a leisurely walk down Main Street, and you'll be enchanted by the quaint shops nestled within historic buildings.

Outlet Malls and Shopping Centers

For those seeking a more extensive shopping experience, Cape Cod boasts several outlet malls and shopping centers where you can find popular brands and great deals.

The Cape Cod Mall, located in Hyannis, is the region's largest shopping destination. It houses a wide range of stores, from well-known retail chains to specialty shops. With a variety of clothing, accessories, electronics, and home goods, the Cape Cod Mall has something for everyone.

If you're a bargain hunter, the Cape Cod Factory Outlets in Sagamore is the place to go. Here, you'll find a collection of outlet stores offering discounted prices on brand-name items. From clothing and shoes to housewares and sportswear, you're sure to find some fantastic deals.

Local Markets and Farmers' Markets

Experience the true essence of Cape Cod by exploring its local markets and farmers' markets. These vibrant markets not only offer an opportunity to support local businesses but also allow you to savor the freshest produce and unique handmade products.

Visit the Cape Cod Farmers' Market in Barnstable, where you'll find a diverse selection of fresh fruits, vegetables, flowers, and artisanal goods. Interact with local farmers, artists, and craftsmen, and gain insights into their craft.

In addition to the farmers' markets, Cape Cod hosts numerous craft fairs and artisan markets throughout the year. Keep an eye out for events like the Hyannis Open-Air Market, where you can browse through stalls offering handmade jewelry, pottery, artwork, and other distinctive items.

Tips for Shopping in Cape Cod

- Support Local: Cape Cod is rich in local talent and businesses. When shopping, opt for locally-made products to support the community and take home unique keepsakes.

- Seasonal Sales: Many stores offer seasonal sales, particularly during the shoulder seasons. Keep an eye out for discounts and promotions that can help you save while shopping.

- Sustainable Choices: Consider eco-friendly products and those made from sustainable materials. Many boutiques and galleries on the Cape prioritize environmentally conscious products.

- Bring Reusable Bags: Embrace the Cape's eco-friendly culture by bringing reusable shopping bags to minimize plastic waste.

- Check Opening Hours: Cape Cod's shopping scene can be more laid-back, with some stores operating on limited hours, especially during the off-season. Plan ahead and check opening times to avoid disappointment.

- Explore Hidden Gems: Don't hesitate to explore lesser-known areas for unique finds. Local art co-ops and off-the-beaten-path shops often harbor treasures waiting to be discovered.

Shopping in Cape Cod is an experience to cherish. From browsing through art galleries to finding one-of-a-kind souvenirs, the Cape offers an enticing array of shopping options. Whether you prefer trendy fashion, handcrafted art, or local produce, there's something for every taste and interest. As you explore the shopping landscape of Cape Cod, remember to support local businesses, embrace sustainability, and enjoy the distinctive charm of this remarkable destination.

CHAPTER 9

RECOMMENDED ITINERARY

Cape Cod offers a diverse range of experiences for visitors, from pristine beaches and charming towns to cultural attractions and outdoor adventures. To make the most of your trip, we've put together three unique itineraries that cater to different interests and durations. Whether you have three days, five days, or a full week, these carefully crafted plans will help you create lasting memories of your Cape Cod adventure.

3-Day Cape Cod Adventure

Day 1: Beach Bliss and Sunset Delight

- Start your day early and head to Coast Guard Beach in the Cape Cod National Seashore. Enjoy a leisurely morning stroll along the shore and take in the breathtaking views of the Atlantic Ocean.

- After working up an appetite, indulge in a classic Cape Cod experience with a seafood lunch at Arnold's Lobster & Clam Bar. Don't forget to try their famous lobster roll!

- In the afternoon, explore the picturesque town of Chatham. Visit the Chatham Lighthouse and observe the stunning scenery from the observation deck.

- Spend the rest of the day at Chatham Bars Inn Beach, known for its tranquil waters and soft sands. Relax, swim, and soak up the sun until the evening.

- For dinner, savor a delightful meal at The Impudent Oyster in Chatham, offering a mix of seafood and international dishes.

- End your first day in Cape Cod by witnessing a mesmerizing sunset at Skaket Beach in Orleans. This bay beach is renowned for its stunning sunset views over Cape Cod Bay.

Day 2: Whale Watching and Provincetown Exploration

- Catch an early morning whale watching tour from Provincetown. The Stellwagen Bank National Marine Sanctuary is a prime spot for spotting humpback whales, dolphins, and other marine life.

- Enjoy a quick brunch in Provincetown's vibrant downtown, filled with artsy boutiques and galleries.

- Visit the iconic Pilgrim Monument, a historic structure that offers a panoramic view of the town and surrounding areas.

- Stroll along Commercial Street and discover unique shops and local artistry.

- For a unique experience, opt for a dune tour in Provincetown's sand dunes. Learn about the region's natural history and enjoy the stunning landscapes.

- In the evening, indulge in fresh seafood at The Lobster Pot, one of Provincetown's oldest and most famous seafood restaurants.

Day 3: Cultural Immersion and Farewell

- Explore the JFK Hyannis Museum in Hyannis, dedicated to the life and times of President John F. Kennedy.

- Take a ferry to Nantucket for a day trip and discover its cobblestone streets, historic homes, and scenic beauty.

- If you prefer to stay on the mainland, spend the afternoon at the Cape Cod Maritime Museum in Hyannis to learn about the Cape's maritime heritage.

- End your journey with a farewell dinner at The Naked Oyster Bistro and Raw Bar, known for its delectable seafood dishes and cozy ambiance.

5-Day Family-Friendly Vacation

Day 1: Beach Day and Family Fun

- Start your family vacation at Mayflower Beach in Dennis, known for its tide pools and gentle waves perfect for kids to play in.

- After a morning of beachcombing and building sandcastles, head to the Cape Cod Inflatable Park in West Yarmouth for an afternoon of water slides, minigolf, and other family-friendly activities.

- Enjoy a relaxed dinner at Captain Parker's Pub, a family-friendly restaurant serving New England comfort food.

Day 2: Nature and Wildlife Adventure

- Begin your day with a visit to the Wellfleet Bay Wildlife Sanctuary. Take a guided nature walk and spot various bird species and other wildlife.

- After a picnic lunch in the sanctuary, head to the Cape Cod Museum of Natural History in Brewster, offering interactive exhibits and educational programs for kids.

- In the late afternoon, visit the Wellfleet Drive-In Theater for a unique movie-watching experience from the comfort of your car.

Day 3: Exploring Chatham and Seal Watching

- Spend the morning at the Chatham Shark Center, an educational center dedicated to sharks and marine conservation.

- Afterward, embark on a seal-watching cruise from Chatham to see these playful creatures in their natural habitat.

- In the afternoon, stroll through the charming town of Chatham and enjoy ice cream at The Lazy Lobster.

Day 4: Adventure and Fun in Hyannis

- Head to the Cape Cod Children's Museum in Mashpee for a morning of interactive exhibits and hands-on activities suitable for kids of all ages.

- For lunch, try a family-friendly restaurant like The Lobster Boat, offering seafood and other kid-friendly options.

- Spend the afternoon at the Cape Codder Water Park in Hyannis, featuring water slides, wave pools, and a lazy river.

- End the day with a delicious dinner at The British Beer Company, offering a diverse menu to satisfy everyone's taste buds.

Day 5: Relaxation and Farewell

- Take a leisurely morning at one of Cape Cod's beautiful beaches, such as Sandy Neck Beach in Barnstable.

- Enjoy a picnic lunch by the water before bidding farewell to Cape Cod.

7-Day Relaxation and Wellness Retreat

Day 1: Arrival and Beachside Relaxation

- Arrive in Cape Cod and settle into your chosen accommodation, such as the serene Wequassett Resort and Golf Club in Chatham.

- Spend the afternoon unwinding at the resort's private beach, indulging in beach yoga or simply basking in the sun.

- For a relaxing dinner, savor the fine dining experience at Twenty-Eight Atlantic, known for its exquisite cuisine and picturesque views of Pleasant Bay.

Day 2: Spa and Nature Retreat

- Treat yourself to a luxurious spa day at one of Cape Cod's top-rated spas, such as The Spa at Chatham Bars Inn.

- In the afternoon, explore the scenic Monomoy National Wildlife Refuge and take a nature walk to rejuvenate your senses.

- End the day with a gourmet seafood dinner at the Chatham Pier Fish Market.

Day 3: Art and Culture Immersion

- Spend the morning visiting the Cape Cod Museum of Art in Dennis, featuring a diverse collection of local and regional artworks.

- After lunch, visit the Heritage Museums & Gardens in Sandwich, known for its beautiful gardens and art exhibits.

- Enjoy a delightful dinner at the Glass Onion in Falmouth, offering a farm-to-table dining experience with a focus on fresh, local ingredients.

Day 4: Relaxing Day at the Resort

- Take a day to fully relax and enjoy the amenities at your resort. Treat yourself to a spa treatment, lounge by the pool, or take a quiet stroll along the resort's private beach.

- For a serene dining experience, opt for a romantic dinner at the Ocean Terrace, offering coastal views and delectable seafood dishes.

Day 5: Biking and Nature Exploration

- Rent bicycles and embark on a scenic ride along the Cape Cod Rail Trail, passing through picturesque landscapes and charming towns.

- Stop for a picnic lunch at Nickerson State Park in Brewster, surrounded by lush forests and freshwater ponds.

- Continue your nature exploration with a leisurely walk along Skaket Beach during low tide, where you can witness captivating tidal pools and wildlife.

Day 6: Cape Cod Winery and Sunset Cruise

- Start your day with a visit to the Truro Vineyards of Cape Cod, where you can savor local wines and enjoy the vineyard's serene ambiance.

- In the afternoon, take a sunset cruise from Provincetown to see the picturesque coastline and possibly spot some marine life.

- Enjoy a farewell dinner at The Red Inn, offering a fine dining experience with stunning views of Provincetown Harbor.

Day 7: Departure

- Depart from Cape Cod with rejuvenated spirits and cherished memories of your relaxation and wellness retreat.

No matter the duration of your Cape Cod trip or your interests, this picturesque region of Massachusetts offers an abundance of experiences to suit every traveler. From stunning beaches and rich cultural heritage to outdoor adventures and relaxation, Cape Cod promises a memorable vacation filled with beauty and serenity. Use these recommended itineraries as a guide to plan your dream getaway and make the most of your time in this charming coastal destination. Happy travels!

CHAPTER 10

TRAVELING WITH PETS

Cape Cod is not just a destination for humans; it's also a fantastic place to bring your furry companions along for the adventure. With its beautiful beaches, pet-friendly parks, and accommodating accommodations, traveling with pets in Cape Cod can be an enjoyable and rewarding experience for both you and your four-legged friends. In this chapter, we'll explore the best practices for bringing pets to Cape Cod, including pet-friendly spots, accommodations, and essential services.

Pet-Friendly Beaches and Parks

When you visit Cape Cod with your pets, you'll be delighted to know that there are several pet-friendly beaches and parks where your furry pals can stretch their legs, play, and splash in the water. Some of the most popular pet-friendly beaches include:

1. **Pilgrim Bark Park**: Located in Provincetown, this off-leash dog park provides a safe and social environment for dogs to run and interact freely. The park is divided into two sections, one for small dogs and the other for larger breeds, ensuring a comfortable experience for all pets.

2. **Drummer Boy Park**: Situated in Brewster, Drummer Boy Park is a welcoming space for leashed dogs to stroll alongside the walking trails and enjoy the lush greenery. The park also hosts various events and festivals throughout the year, making it a lively spot for both pets and their owners.

3. **Sandy Neck Beach**: This scenic beach in Barnstable allows leashed dogs to accompany their owners on the shore during specific hours. It's a great place for long walks and stunning views of the Atlantic Ocean.

Remember to always check the specific rules and regulations for each pet-friendly beach or park you plan to visit, as some areas might have restrictions or seasonal changes.

Pet-Friendly Accommodations

Finding the right pet-friendly accommodation is crucial for a stress-free stay in Cape Cod. Fortunately, many hotels, inns, and rental properties warmly welcome pets. Here are some top-rated pet-friendly accommodations:

1. **Paws A While**: This charming bed and breakfast in Chatham cater exclusively to guests with pets. They offer comfortable rooms and a lovely garden where pets can roam and play.

2. **Doggy Dreamhouse**: Located in Provincetown, Doggy Dreamhouse is a pet-friendly vacation rental that provides ample space for both you and your furry friends to relax and enjoy your vacation together.

3. **Cape Cod Ocean Manor**: Situated right on the beach in Dennis Port, Cape Cod Ocean Manor offers pet-friendly cottages with stunning ocean views, perfect for a memorable family vacation with your pets.

When booking accommodation, make sure to inform the property in advance about your pets and any specific requirements you might have. Additionally, check if there are any additional fees or pet policies that apply.

Local Pet Services

While in Cape Cod, you'll find several convenient pet services to ensure your pets' needs are well taken care of during your stay. From veterinary clinics to pet groomers and pet supply stores, Cape Cod has you covered. Here are some essential pet services:

1. **Cape Cod Animal Hospital**: With multiple locations across the Cape, the Cape Cod Animal Hospital provides comprehensive veterinary care for

your pets, including routine check-ups, vaccinations, and emergency services.

2. **Paws & Whiskers**: This pet supply store in Hyannis offers a wide range of pet products, from premium pet food and treats to toys and accessories, ensuring your pets stay happy and comfortable during your vacation.

3. **PetSmart**: Located in Barnstable, PetSmart is another excellent option for pet supplies and services, offering grooming services and a wide selection of pet products for dogs, cats, and other small animals.

Always keep your pets' health and well-being in mind while exploring Cape Cod. Make sure they are properly hydrated, have access to shade, and avoid walking them on hot pavements during peak sun hours. Additionally, keep a leash on your pet while in public places, even in designated pet-friendly areas, to ensure the safety and comfort of all visitors.

Traveling with pets to Cape Cod can be a rewarding experience for both you and your furry companions. From exploring pet-friendly beaches and parks to staying in welcoming accommodations and accessing essential pet services, Cape Cod offers a warm and inviting environment for pets of all kinds. Remember to plan ahead, follow local rules and regulations, and prioritize your pets' well-being throughout your vacation. With the right preparation and a sense of adventure, you and your pets are sure to create cherished memories on the beautiful shores of Cape Cod. Happy travels!

CHAPTER 11

SAFETY AND EMERGENCY INFORMATION

Cape Cod is a beautiful and inviting destination, but like any travel location, it's essential to be prepared for any unforeseen circumstances. This chapter provides important safety and emergency information to ensure your trip remains safe and enjoyable. From medical facilities and emergency contacts to weather preparedness, we've got you covered.

Local Hospitals and Medical Facilities

While exploring Cape Cod, your health and well-being are of utmost importance. Should you require medical attention, the region offers several excellent hospitals and medical facilities. Here are some notable options:

1. Cape Cod Hospital: Address: 27 Park St, Hyannis, MA 02601 Contact: +1 (508) 771-1800

Cape Cod Hospital is the largest medical facility in the area and provides a comprehensive range of services, including emergency care, surgery, and specialized treatments. The hospital is staffed with skilled medical professionals, ensuring you receive top-notch care during your stay.

2. Falmouth Hospital: Address: 100 Ter Heun Dr, Falmouth, MA 02540 Contact: +1 (508) 548-5300

Falmouth Hospital is located in the charming town of Falmouth and offers excellent medical services to both residents and visitors. It includes emergency care, diagnostic imaging, and various outpatient services.

3. Martha's Vineyard Hospital: Address: 1 Hospital Rd, Oak Bluffs, MA 02557 Contact: +1 (508) 693-0410

For those venturing to Martha's Vineyard, this hospital provides medical care to the island's residents and tourists alike. They offer emergency services and essential medical treatments.

Emergency Contacts

Knowing the correct emergency contacts can make a significant difference in critical situations. Save these numbers in your phone and be prepared to use them if needed:

1. Police, Fire, Medical Emergency: 911

For any life-threatening situation, immediately call 911. The emergency operators will dispatch the appropriate authorities to your location.

2. Cape Cod Police Departments:

- Barnstable Police Department: Contact: +1 (508) 775-0387

- Falmouth Police Department: Contact: +1 (508) 457-2527

- Provincetown Police Department: Contact: +1 (508) 487-1212

3. Poison Control Center: 1-800-222-1222

If you suspect poisoning or need advice on handling toxic substances, call the Poison Control Center for immediate assistance.

4. Coast Guard Search and Rescue: 1-508-457-3211

For maritime emergencies along Cape Cod's coast, contact the U.S. Coast Guard Search and Rescue.

11.3 Weather and Natural Disaster Preparedness

Cape Cod's weather can be unpredictable, so it's crucial to stay informed and prepared for potential natural disasters. Here's what you need to know:

1. Hurricane Preparedness:

Cape Cod is susceptible to hurricanes and tropical storms, especially during the Atlantic hurricane season from June to November. If you're visiting during this period, keep an eye on weather updates and be ready to follow evacuation orders if necessary.

- Familiarize yourself with the evacuation routes in your area.

- Have an emergency kit ready, including essential supplies like water, non-perishable food, flashlights, and first aid items.

- Secure outdoor furniture and objects that could become projectiles in strong winds.

2. Rip Current Awareness:

Cape Cod's beaches can experience rip currents, which are powerful and potentially dangerous water currents. Always adhere to the lifeguards' instructions and posted warning signs. If caught in a rip current, swim parallel to the shore until you break free of its pull.

3. Thunderstorms and Lightning:

During summer months, thunderstorms with lightning are common. Seek shelter indoors if a thunderstorm approaches, and avoid staying outside until the storm has passed.

4. Winter Storms:

Winter storms can bring heavy snow and icy conditions to Cape Cod. If you're visiting during the winter, monitor weather forecasts and take necessary precautions when traveling on icy roads.

Remember, it's essential to stay informed about local weather conditions and any potential hazards during your stay in Cape Cod. Follow the advice of local authorities and take appropriate measures to ensure your safety.

Overall, while Cape Cod is a paradise for travelers, being prepared for emergencies and knowing how to respond to unforeseen situations is crucial. Familiarize yourself with local medical facilities, save emergency contacts, and stay informed about weather conditions. With proper planning and precautions, you can enjoy a worry-free and memorable experience on this picturesque peninsula.

CHAPTER 12

SUSTAINABLE TRAVEL TIPS

As you embark on your journey to explore the natural beauty and charming towns of Cape Cod, it's essential to be mindful of the impact you have on the environment and local communities. Sustainable travel practices can help preserve the region's unique ecosystems, support local businesses, and ensure that future generations can also enjoy the wonders of this coastal paradise. In this chapter, we'll delve into some valuable sustainable travel tips that will enhance your Cape Cod experience while minimizing your ecological footprint.

Responsible Tourism Practices

1. Respect Wildlife and Nature: Cape Cod is home to a diverse range of wildlife, including endangered species and fragile ecosystems. When visiting natural areas, maintain a safe distance from animals and refrain from feeding or touching them. Stick to marked trails and avoid trampling on sensitive vegetation.

2. Reduce Plastic Usage: Plastic pollution poses a significant threat to marine life. Help combat this issue by using reusable water bottles, bags, and containers during your trip. Many establishments in Cape Cod

support sustainable initiatives by offering alternatives to single-use plastics.

3. Conserve Water: Cape Cod summers can get hot, leading to an increased demand for water. Be mindful of your water usage, especially during times of drought. Consider taking shorter showers and reusing towels to minimize water consumption at accommodations.

4. Support Local Conservation Efforts: Various organizations on Cape Cod are dedicated to protecting the environment and wildlife. Consider supporting them through donations, volunteer work, or by participating in eco-friendly tours that contribute to conservation efforts.

Eco-Friendly Activities and Tours

1. Kayaking and Stand-Up Paddleboarding: Explore Cape Cod's scenic waterways while minimizing your impact on the environment. Kayaking and stand-up paddleboarding are eco-friendly ways to enjoy the coastline, and they provide opportunities for wildlife sightings without disturbing the habitats.

2. Eco-Tours and Nature Walks: Join guided eco-tours and nature walks led by knowledgeable local experts.

These tours emphasize the region's ecology and cultural heritage, promoting a deeper understanding of Cape Cod's natural wonders.

3. Whale Watching with Responsible Operators: Cape Cod is renowned for its whale-watching opportunities. Choose tour operators that prioritize responsible practices, such as maintaining a safe distance from marine life and following guidelines to protect whales and other sea creatures.

4. Bike Tours: Instead of driving, consider exploring Cape Cod's towns and scenic routes by bicycle. Many areas have well-maintained bike paths, providing a leisurely and eco-friendly way to experience the region.

Reduce, Reuse, and Recycle in Cape Cod

1. Recycling: Cape Cod communities are committed to recycling efforts. Familiarize yourself with local recycling guidelines and dispose of recyclables appropriately. Opt for accommodations that offer recycling facilities and make a conscious effort to reduce waste.

2. Sustainable Shopping: Choose to shop at stores and markets that support local artisans, sell eco-friendly

products, or use sustainable packaging. Support businesses that prioritize environmental responsibility.

3. Minimize Food Waste: Cape Cod's culinary scene offers a delectable array of seafood and locally sourced produce. When dining out, be mindful of portion sizes to minimize food waste. If you have leftovers, consider taking them back to your accommodation or asking for composting options.

4. Energy Conservation: Help reduce energy consumption by turning off lights, electronics, and air conditioning when not in use. Choose accommodations that practice energy-saving initiatives and use renewable energy sources whenever possible.

By embracing sustainable travel practices during your visit to Cape Cod, you can be a positive force in preserving this captivating coastal region. From respecting wildlife and reducing plastic usage to supporting local conservation efforts and engaging in eco-friendly activities, your responsible choices will contribute to the long-term health and well-being of Cape Cod's natural environment and local communities. By leaving only footprints and taking cherished memories, you'll be making a difference and ensuring that future travelers can also revel in the timeless beauty of Cape Cod. Happy and responsible travels!

Conclusion

Your Unforgettable Cape Cod Experience

As your journey through Cape Cod comes to an end, you can undoubtedly reflect on the unique and captivating experiences you've had in this charming destination. From the picturesque beaches of the Cape Cod National Seashore to the vibrant streets of Provincetown and the tranquil landscapes of Chatham, Cape Cod offers something for every traveler. This Conclusion chapter aims to summarize your memorable adventure, offer final thoughts, and inspire you to return to this idyllic coastal region.

Throughout this travel guide, we have explored the best places to visit, diverse accommodation options, delectable local cuisine, and engaging outdoor activities. Whether you followed the suggested itineraries or forged your path, Cape Cod surely left a lasting impression on your heart.

Fond Farewell and Happy Travels!

As you bid farewell to Cape Cod, take with you the cherished memories of breathtaking sunsets, the refreshing sea breeze, and the warmth of the locals. Cape Cod's unique blend of natural beauty, rich history, and cultural diversity ensures that visitors from all walks of life find something to love.

Remember to embrace the spirit of the Cape and carry it with you wherever your travels take you. Cape Cod's allure lies not only in its physical beauty but also in the laid-back lifestyle and the genuine hospitality of its residents. Share your experiences with family and friends, as there is no doubt that you will inspire others to venture on their Cape Cod adventure.

We hope this travel guide has been your trusted companion, providing valuable insights and tips for a seamless trip. But beyond the pages of this guide, there are countless hidden gems awaiting discovery. Don't hesitate to explore beyond the well-known spots and seek out the quieter corners of Cape Cod, where you might stumble upon your most cherished moments.

As you return home, consider keeping a piece of Cape Cod with you—a seashell from your favorite beach, a piece of artwork from a local gallery, or a treasured recipe of a Cape Cod specialty. These tokens will serve as reminders of the magic you experienced and inspire you to return someday.

The Spirit of Cape Cod

Cape Cod's allure is timeless and ever-evolving, driven by a deep-rooted appreciation for nature, art, and community.

It is a place where you can find solace and rejuvenate your spirit, where creativity thrives, and where simple pleasures become extraordinary.

Beyond the hustle and bustle of everyday life, Cape Cod offers a sanctuary where you can slow down, breathe in the fresh ocean air, and immerse yourself in the wonders of nature. The soft sand beneath your feet, the sound of crashing waves, and the sight of soaring seagulls will forever echo in your mind.

While this guide provided you with valuable information, remember that Cape Cod's essence lies in embracing its essence on a personal level. Take the time to connect with the locals, savor the local cuisine, and listen to the tales of the region's history.

Sustaining Cape Cod's Beauty

As a responsible traveler, you have the power to contribute positively to the preservation of Cape Cod's natural beauty and unique charm. Consider adopting sustainable travel practices during your visit and supporting local businesses that prioritize eco-friendly initiatives.

Take care to leave no trace during your outdoor adventures, dispose of waste responsibly, and respect the wildlife and delicate ecosystems that thrive in this area. By being mindful of your actions, you play a crucial role in ensuring that future generations can also enjoy the wonders of Cape Cod.

Until We Meet Again

While this chapter marks the end of your Cape Cod travel guide, it does not signify the end of your connection with this captivating destination. Keep the memories alive through stories, photographs, and shared experiences with others.

When the time comes for your next adventure, Cape Cod will warmly welcome you back, ready to reveal new secrets and surprises. As the seasons change and the landscapes transform, Cape Cod's allure remains eternal, beckoning you to return and create even more treasured memories.

Safe travels and until we meet again on the shores of Cape Cod!

Printed in Great Britain
by Amazon

38798444R00046